Jacqueline Kennedy Onassis

A TRIBUTE

Jacqueline Kennedy Onassis

The Making of a First Lady

A TRIBUTE
by Jacques Lowe

GPG
GENERAL
PUBLISHING
GROUP, INC

A
JACQUES LOWE
VISUAL ARTS PROJECTS
BOOK

Publisher: W. Quay Hays
Editor: Peter L. Hoffman

For information:
General Publishing Group, Inc.
2701 Ocean Park Boulevard
Santa Monica, CA 90405

Library of Congress Cataloging-in-Publication Data
Lowe, Jacques.
    Jacqueline Kennedy Onassis : the making of a first lady /
tribute by Jacques Lowe ; introduction by Letitia Baldridge.
        p. cm.
        ISBN 1-881649-78-4
        1. Onassis, Jacqueline Kennedy, 1929–1994. 2. Presidents'
spouses—United States—Biography. 3. Celebrities—United
States—Biography. I. Title.
E843.K4L69 1996
973.922'092—dc20
[B]   96-751
                                                          CIP

Book design by Joseph Guglietti
Printed in Italy
10 9 8 7 6 5 4 3 2 1

General Publishing Group
Los Angeles

Contents

Foreword

I knew Jackie from the time we were both teenagers living in the Washington area. I was just ahead of her at Miss Porter's School in Farmington, Connecticut, and then at Vassar. When I started my first job at the American embassy in Paris, she arrived on the scene as a student at the Sorbonne. There was no way then to predict that within a decade she would be following the yellow brick road to the White House.

To meet her, even during her adolescent years, was never to forget her. She was a natural beauty—wearing none of the trappings of the teenage cosmetic fashions of the day. There were no globs of neon purple lipstick, no thick eyebrows blackened with strokes of a dark pencil. Nor did her skin suffocate under a thick layer of Pan-Cake makeup. Even more important to me in my earliest impression of this young girl was her voice—unforgettable in its soft, breathy tones. It was a sound that forced one to draw close and listen well.

She was born with a built-in fashion flair. So was her sister Lee Radziwill (it must have been in the Bouvier genes). That sense of style governed not only what she bought but the way she wore it. She frequently received letters from women who complained that they had purchased "exact copies" of the First Lady's outfits (usually mass-produced and in the marketplace six weeks after Jackie appeared in them), but "When I put on the dress, the effect isn't as dazzling." They simply could not understand why, if they were the same size, roughly the same age and clad in the same outfit, they did not look just like Jackie.

She received thousands of letters each week brimming with other questions. Nothing, it seemed, was too personal to ask: What is your diet? What do the children (and their animals!) eat? What brand of toothbrush do you use ("those wonderful teeth," they would exclaim in their letters)?

Jackie looked radiant that summer when JFK captured his party's presidential nomination. This is my favorite portrait of her. Although wearing a simple summer dress, devoid of jewelry or any other accouterments, she looks regal and serene, and astonishingly beautiful. She exudes inner strength and a certainty of purpose. No wonder many Americans admired and imitated her, and called her a queen.

HYANNIS PORT, MASSACHUSETTS. SUMMER 1960

And even, What laxative do you and the President take, because, as one correspondent concluded, "You look like regular people."

The letters I most liked to read were those that simply showed the writer's admiration for the First Lady and asked for nothing in return: "The happy, beautiful look on your children's faces shows what a good mother you are" and "I tried putting some lilies of the valley in an antique porcelain mug in an unexpected corner of our living room, like I saw you had done in a photograph, and my husband and I look at it all the time. It's so beautiful—how wonderful you are to have things around you like that!"

Of course, they're gone now—the John F. Kennedys and their White House magic. The American public did not wish it to end, that allure and romance. But now there's a closure, and complaints are being heard throughout the land that people didn't know Jackie well enough during those White House years and after; even members of the younger generation who weren't around in the 1960s can't get enough of her today.

During the Kennedy administration Pam Turnure stood guarding her boss' privacy as Jackie's efficient press secretary; toward the end Nancy Tuckerman took over as White House social secretary, becoming the First Lady's lifelong and most trusted aide-de-camp. Whatever the world was able to learn about Jackie through her official duties and obvious devotion to her children, I don't think the public ever realized just how much she helped her husband behind the scenes.

Jackie would leave cartoons and limericks for Jack in unexpected places to cheer him up when the nation's affairs were going badly. She would arrange for special treats (like Joe's Stone Crabs from Miami and his favorite ice cream) to be served when he was under unusually great pressure in the Oval Office. With deft timing, old friends would pay morale-boosting calls

This family portrait was taken for the 1960 Christmas card. Jackie loved the picture, but wondered whether it was possible to replace Caroline's head with one from another frame which she preferred. I tried, but it was technically impossible. She finally decided to go ahead with this original.

HYANNIS PORT, MASSACHUSETTS. AUGUST 1960

at Jackie's prompting. But her most effective weapon in raising Jack's spirits was a surprise visit to his office with the children. And she labored more over his birthday celebrations than over any state dinner.

Many days she would be waiting by the elevator to the family apartment to help him when he emerged from it, dragging himself on crutches and in excruciating back pain. It was a sight the President would not have wanted outsiders to witness.

It's hard work being "First Lady," a title Jackie hated. Initially, she instructed her staff to refer to her as "Mrs. Kennedy," but that didn't last long. Tradition is a tough wrestling partner. Whether she was hosting an event for 2,000 people in ninety-degree heat in the backyard, as she once sarcastically described the South Lawn, or watching a cobra fight a mongoose to death (as Indian protocol dictated she do in Prime Minister Nehru's garden), she was ever the trouper.

People have never stopped talking about her manners. Jackie learned those as every young woman does—as a little girl, from her mother. Her handwritten notes were beautiful—not only in their warm, affectionate style but in their frequency and timing. The morning after a dinner, the day after a bouquet was received, out a note would go, with its simply engraved "The White House" heading the stationery.

Sometimes in those notes—and virtually everywhere else—there would be glimpses of her humor. She sought the fun in any situation and seemed to have a continually amused sparkle in her eye—even while holding others at a distance. Washington saw much mimicking and limerick-spouting at parties during the Kennedy years. The popular French ambassador, Hervè Alphand, for example, was famous for performing his imitations of world leaders as after-dinner entertainment at the French

This photograph was taken the first time I ever met Jack and Jackie Kennedy. We had earlier taken a formal portrait in the library that was to serve as a Christmas card, and I asked that we repeat a more relaxed group portrait on the porch. Caroline instinctively reached for her mother's pearls and put them in her mouth. The image, perhaps because of its innocence and simplicity, has become an icon.

HYANNIS PORT, MASSACHUSETTS. SUMMER 1958

embassy. Jackie is the only person I have known who could imitate Ambassador Alphand imitating President Charles de Gaulle. (Even Robin Williams would have a hard time doing that.)

Witty, bright, generous of spirit: Those enduring qualities form a mental scrapbook of endless pages. But as the future begins to slip by even more quickly than the past, what will my overriding memory of Jackie be? As the regal chatelaine of the Number One House of the land (make that the world)? When somebody dies, one tends to remember a definitive image of that person. Mine will certainly not be the one television gave us of her coffin about to be lowered into the earth at Arlington National Cemetery—a casket shining so cleanly and peacefully in the sun, decorated so tastefully with greenery on the top, centered with a simple white cross of flowers.

No, my image through the years ahead will be of her in the white silk Givenchy ball gown she wore during a 1961 state visit to France for the farewell dinner President and Madame de Gaulle hosted in the Hall of Mirrors in Versailles. The top of her white dress was a veritable painting of pastel flowers, all hand-embroidered in paillettes. The President was unbelievably handsome that night in his white tie and tails. Jackie and Jack looked at one another with open admiration as they left Paris arm in arm for Versailles. They were, after all, a team, and this balmy June evening was a far cry from the campaign trail back home. The air around them was literally charged with electricity from the synergy of their presence, physical appearance, talent and youth. The de Gaulles and every other guest at that large formal dinner were transfixed by the two of them all evening long.

We watched a ballet commissioned by Louis XV himself. It was more than magical. It was a dream sequence for every member of the White

In 1959 John F. Kennedy's campaign for the democratic presidential nomination began in earnest, although he wouldn't announce his entry officially for another year. Jackie in those early days was often at his side, amusing herself on these long trips with needlework, crocheting and quilting, as she is doing here.

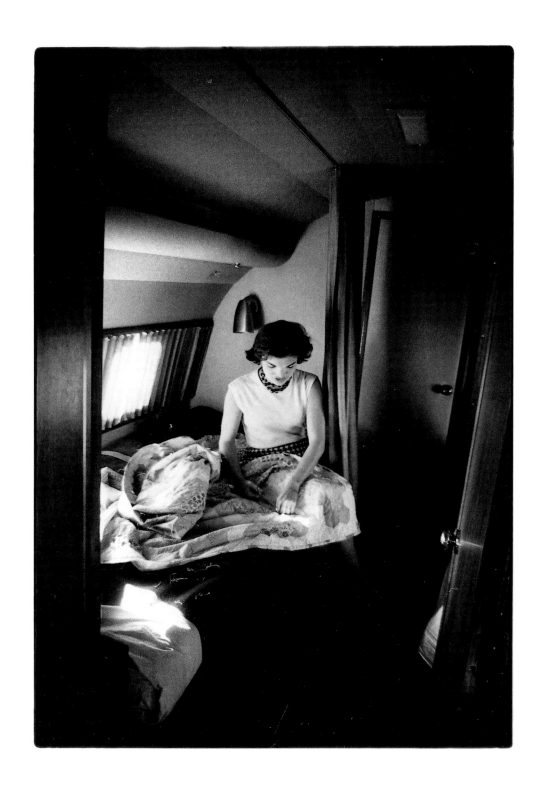

CALIFORNIA. SPRING 1960

House party who was fortunate enough to be present. No one enjoyed or appreciated it more than John and Jacqueline Kennedy.

When the evening was over and the single file of limousines wound its way back to Paris through the beautifully lit gardens and allèes of trees in the Parc de Versailles, we suddenly heard the American and then the French national anthems over loudspeakers. The Kennedys stopped the procession and got out of their car. No one would have dared follow them. They walked alone to a giant, illuminated fountain as the music continued playing through the trees. They stood hand in hand in silence, savoring this moment in history for at least five minutes, their figures silhouetted against the fountain's dancing, flickering waters. I was not the only one to hold my breath.

That is the image I will always take with me: of the two of them, the Presidential team, hand in hand, giving a premier performance on a state visit to a foreign land, doing us proud.

Utter perfection. Taste and grace.

Letitia Baldridge

MRS. BALDRIDGE WAS JACQUELINE KENNEDY'S SOCIAL SECRETARY IN THE KENNEDY WHITE HOUSE

The early days of the campaign were very relaxed, even fun. The Senator was surrounded by his wife, a few friends and perhaps two or three campaign aides. Stopping off, often in very small towns, the crowds could be counted in the dozens, unlike the tens of thousands who would show up a year later. Jackie was happy then to give interviews to all who asked. Here she prepares for a radio chat at a small town station in California.

CALIFORNIA. SPRING 1960

Introduction

She has been called the world's most beautiful woman. Aristocratic and regal, much admired for her style, her bearing and her strength in the face of adversity, she has become a model for motherhood, independence and beauty. Yet when analyzing these pictures we realize that she wasn't a perfect beauty. To a beauty editor her eyes would be too irregular, her jaw too strong, her mouth too large, her nose flawed. But the aggregate result is that of a woman we can only call "stunning." It was her inner beauty and strength, her near royal bearing, her quiet intelligence that people saw and reacted to, that made her the near mythical figure she has become in the eyes of the world, even in the eyes of her detractors.

Her ability to transform herself from a debutante to First Lady of the land, and finally to a working editor, earned her the respect of many who may have been skeptical about her intelligence, creative ability and personal values. As a leading influence and promoter of the arts and all things aesthetic while in the White House, she won the undying gratitude of America's—and the world's—artists and intellectuals.

When she returned to New York after her years in self-exile, she continued to be a major influence upon all things artistic, not only through the beautiful books she helped publish and the worthwhile causes she lent her name to and rigorously pursued—such as helping save New York's landmark buildings from destruction, Grand Central Station among them—but through the very force of her gentle personality. Private and at times reclusive, she continued to fascinate and remained a symbol to men and women, to the young who had no recollection of the Kennedy years as well as to the old, to Americans and citizens of the world.

I admired her greatly. Her loss was a very personal one, both to those who knew her and to the many who only saw her from afar.

Senator Kennedy, Jackie and Caroline pose for a portrait in their N Street townhouse. That portrait was my first cover assignment from a major magazine. Kennedy still was one of seven unannounced presidential candidates. The contest had not yet begun in earnest.

GEORGETOWN. FALL 1959

I

As a young photojournalist in the summer of 1956, I was freelancing for a number of publications. Through my work I met Robert F. Kennedy, who had recently been appointed majority counsel to the United States Senate's McClellan Committee, otherwise known as the Labor Racket's Committee. From the beginning the young lawyer had made a name for himself through his tough and relentless questioning of labor racketeers such as Dave Beck, president of the Teamster's Union, and Jimmy Hoffa, his heir apparent. "Bobby" had become an overnight celebrity in Washington, D.C.

I had been assigned by a magazine called *The Sign* to go down to Washington and photograph the young firebrand, and we got along quite well. Returning that Monday evening to my home in New York, I received an assignment from a second magazine to photograph Bobby two days later, on Wednesday. Bobby had the magazine's name on his calendar, not the photographer, so when I walked in there was much ribbing about my wearing two different hats, and we had another excellent photo session. I left that night with a promise to send some pictures. The next day, a Thursday, I had an urgent call from *Collier's* magazine for yet another Bobby Kennedy photo session. It had been set up for the next day, a Friday.

When I showed up for the third time in that week representing yet another magazine, an astonished Bobby Kennedy invited me to dinner at his home after the session, and when it got late, invited me to stay overnight, an offer I gladly accepted. While there I took some pictures of Bobby and Ethel, his wife and their then five children over dinner, a lively gathering full of discussion. Later the children and their parents knelt down for their nightly prayers and the evening ended in a spirited pillow fight. The next morning I promised pictures again and left. It was to be the beginning of a long and fateful friendship.

While few adults had started caring about the Kennedy campaign in early 1959, high-school students welcomed the Kennedys much more openly and less critically, given the candidate's youth and self-deprecating wit, and his wife's ease and elegance. The problem with these high-school meetings was that none of the kids were old enough to vote, but in some towns it was difficult to find anyone willing to shake the hand of the candidate.

CALIFORNIA. SPRING 1960

Over the next twelve months, Bobby and Ethel invited my family to spend some weekends at their home in McLean, Virginia, and later in the summer of 1957, we were their guests at their summer home in Hyannis Port, Massachusetts, at the now famous Kennedy compound. For this young photographer, these weekends were a magnificent photo opportunity. Not only were Bobby's own children romping about together with dozens of kids—friends of the different Kennedy children—but animals of every description roamed the premises—including dogs, cats, ponies, donkeys and horses. The activity was breathtaking, ranging from tennis games and pool parties to muscular football and softball games, interrupted only by outdoor barbecues consisting of hot dogs, hamburgers and the normal all-American fare. The competition may have been fierce, but the resulting photographs were very rewarding. It was a photographer's paradise.

In the early summer of 1957 I sent Bobby a set of large prints chronicling the year's activities. It was my way of saying "thanks." He was on the phone in a flash, full of praise and admiration for the pictures, asking for another set. I told him he was nuts. What was he going to do with all these pictures? After all, I had sent 128 prints. He said they were to be a birthday present for his father. I made the prints and forgot all about it.

Two months later, the phone rang at midnight and the speaker said, "Mr. Lowe, this is Joe Kennedy." Ambassador Kennedy was a near mythical figure at the time and, knowing that some of my friends knew that Bobby had become a friend, I suspected a prank. "Sure," I said, "This is Santa Claus." "No, no, this is Joe Kennedy. Today is my birthday. And Bobby gave me your set of pictures as a present. They're the most wonderful pictures of my family I've ever seen, and the greatest birthday present I ever got. I'm calling to say 'thank you' and to ask you to come

Jackie poses with Caroline on the sun porch in Hyannis Port for some international magazine covers.

GEORGETOWN. SPRING 1959

23

and photograph 'my other son'." I agreed to call Mr. Kennedy at his office the following week. It was the beginning of a long journey.

I called the Ambassador, convinced that he had forgotten all about me, but he did remember, and we made a date to meet in Hyannis Port on a Sunday in July. The other son turned out to be the young Senator from Massachusetts, John F. Kennedy, "Jack."

So on a beautiful summer day in 1958 I drove up to Cape Cod from New York and was greeted by a delighted Joe Kennedy, a very grouchy and almost rude Senator Kennedy, a very gracious Jacqueline Kennedy and their adorable young daughter Caroline.

I was aware that JFK was running for reelection to his Massachusetts Senate seat, but I didn't know how hard he was running. He had just returned from a ten-day campaign trip, was home that weekend and was leaving again the next day for another five-day trip. The last person he wanted to see on this one day of rest was a photographer, but like a dutiful son he was ready for the pictures, wearing a dark blue pin-striped suit on that Sunday instead of his usual Cape Cod weekend garb of slacks and a polo shirt. I, of course, was curious about why he was campaigning so hard, since the papers were filled with predictions that young Senator Kennedy was one of the few Democrats that year who was certain to be reelected. Unbeknownst to me, of course, Jack was already running for President and needed a major win in his home state in order to become a viable candidate. He did get his landslide, and with it, the credibility he needed to be taken seriously.

Jackie, elegantly dressed in a light forest-green, shiny silk dress with a square-cut neck, a triple-strand pearl necklace and pearl earrings, looked stunning. She was gracious and curious about my work and I soon found

The Kennedys arrive at a pre–primary trip in Wisconsin, JFK wearing as usual no hat, coat or gloves on a very cold day.

WISCONSIN. SPRING 1960

25

out that her interest in the creative aspects of photography was very profound (she eventually helped found New York's renowned photography museum, The International Center of Photography).

She had dressed Caroline, then about seven or eight months old, in a white linen dress, frilled at the top, with short puff sleeves, and had styled the baby's hair in what could have passed as a professional coiffure. Both mother and child looked radiant. After struggling to remove the gloom from the senator's face and demeanor and letting in some sunshine, and after trying with difficulty to engage in a dialogue while taking his formal portrait, Jackie's appearance with Caroline finally lightened the atmosphere. The Senator succumbed to the playfulness of his daughter, forgetting the camera for a moment, and when it came time for a portrait of all three, he had relaxed completely. A memorable group photograph in color, with Caroline reaching for her mother's pearls and chewing on them, came out of that session, as did their 1958 Christmas card. I finally felt my trip was a success in spite of the difficult beginning, and Jackie was responsible for that happy outcome.

I stayed for a dinner of Boston clam chowder and a steak and was put up for the night. Next morning by 7:00 A.M. the Senator had already left for his next campaign swing.

An early portrait of Jackie in the Kennedy's Georgetown townhouse.

GEORGETOWN. SPRING 1959

27

II

I didn't hear from JFK or Jackie for weeks after the session. I had sent the contact sheets and some selected prints to their home in Georgetown, and when there was no reaction I began to have doubts about the photo session. Perhaps Kennedy had considered the session a failure. But then, again shortly before midnight, I received my first call from the Senator, as usual dialing his own phone, something I would later get used to. (When he became President, JFK would often avoid the White House switchboard. He would impatiently dial his own phone, especially when he was distracted. I didn't receive many calls like that, but was the recipient of a well–chosen few. The normal call would be, "Mr. Lowe? This is the White House calling. The President would like to speak to you." On these occasions I'd pick up the phone and the familiar voice would come on, "Jacques? This is the President. Why in…did you give that picture to the *New York Times*?" was one call. My sin had been to release a picture of the President with his glasses on his head. It was a striking photo that had been used many times without causing a problem. But he never held a grudge, and there would be no lingering blame. It was nerve-racking, though, to hear the President's irritated voice without the buffer of a switchboard. Jackie was never that emotional.)

He was in Manhattan, he had the pictures with him, he was leaving New York early in the morning and could I come up to the Margery, now? The Margery was a huge apartment complex, then owned by the Kennedy family, encompassing an entire city block on Park Avenue between 48th and 49th Streets, where the family kept some apartments for their personal use. When I knocked, the Senator came to the door dressed only in a towel, having just stepped out of the shower. As I entered, Jackie's voice rang out from a distance, accompanied by water

Jackie in Caroline's nursery at the Kennedy's Georgetown town-house at 3307 N Street.

GEORGETOWN. SPRING 1959

29

splashing and swishing. "Is that you, Jacques?" "Yes." "I really loved your pictures, they're wonderful." "Thank you, I'm very glad about that."

The Senator guided me to a low glass coffee table sitting in the middle of the huge living room and spread out the contacts and prints I had sent. He apologized profusely about his sour mood at the time we photographed and expressed amazement at how I was able to get such marvelous pictures out of a "difficult" session. Jackie, in her bathtub, listened to every word, chiming in with more praise. I was somewhat startled, nervous really, for this was only our second encounter and I hadn't expected such an easy, relaxed atmosphere.

Jack was sitting on the couch and I was on the floor as we discussed the photographs. And the water in the bathroom never stopped splashing as Jackie shouted out specifics as to purpose and print size and the framing of photographs. Eventually, after about an hour and a half, I walked away with a large print order. Jackie never came out to greet me that day. All I remember is the voice and the water splashing, and the Senator in his towel. In retrospect that meeting was hilarious, especially since I seemed to be the only one to notice the almost surrealistic atmosphere, but at the time I was slightly shaken.

Riding piggy-back was one of Caroline's favorite games.

HYANNIS PORT, MASSACHUSETTS. SUMMER 1961

III

B y the spring of 1959 the Kennedys had asked me to take some more photographs of them, this time at their home in Georgetown. I also had several magazine requests for photographs of the Kennedys. Their fame had spread, and magazines had become aware that I had a good relationship with them. So I went to Georgetown for the better part of a week, fulfilling the various magazine assignments as well as Jackie's own requests for pictures.

This time the Senator was still very businesslike, although not gloomy and a great deal friendlier. I spent a day with him alone at the office, following his official routine, and after a while he began to forget about me, ignoring my presence. It was to be like that for the rest of our professional relationship, and an understanding arose between us that I would work and observe almost like a fly on the wall. I was to capture many remarkable, natural and unselfconscious moments of JFK the Senator, presidential candidate and President.

Jackie was extremely gracious, welcoming and quite prepared for the photography sessions when I arrived at the Georgetown house. There were certain photographs the magazines wanted that I had to get. Some were of Jackie posing in different outfits, around the house or sitting at her desk, a small French antique secretaire. She posed with ease, obliging all requests without complaint, even when a particular gown seemed too elegant or elaborate to wear at such an informal session. Some of the picture requests called for "at home" sessions of Jackie and the Senator sitting at the breakfast table, dining with friends or working on Senate business together late at night. Jackie set up all these sessions, at times talking her husband into posing for certain pictures he was loathe to agree to. And of course most of the requests involved his wife with his daughter because both American and European magazines were already fascinated by the fact

The peaceful, idyllic, almost poetic scene in Hyannis Port soon gave way to more frantic commotion as the general election campaign got on its way.

HYANNIS PORT, MASSACHUSETTS. SUMMER 1960

that a woman as stylish as Jackie was also a loving and devoted mother. And she posed freely and at length with her daughter, unencumbered by her later concerns for privacy. In fact her relationship with Caroline, even in front of the camera, was so genuine that I realized that motherhood was her most all-consuming role. When she was with her child, she wasn't posing.

I also tried to follow Jackie's day, which was taken up by a great deal of correspondence with friends and family, the planning of dinner parties and acceptance or rejection of invitations. The young couple was obviously in great demand on Washington's party circuit. Jackie used small white monogrammed notecards with ready envelopes for formal acceptances or invitations, but most of her correspondence was written on a very thin and distinct blue note paper, a paper she used until the end of her days. Her little desk was tucked into the side of the living room, and it served as her office.

Jackie was also quite involved in charitable work. She sometimes worked jointly with the Kennedy sisters, especially JFK's youngest sister, Jean Smith, currently the United States ambassador to Ireland. Both sisters-in-law were very active in organizations dealing with orphans and foster home care, and Jackie set aside two afternoons a week for these charitable causes. With Jean, she would visit foster homes and institutions to see firsthand what these unfortunate children needed to better their lives. For the first time, I observed how tender she could be and how deeply she would involve herself in other people's—total strangers'—lives and problems. There was genuine caring there.

Several times a week she would also join the Senator at his office, working with him on constituency problems. She would help him respond to the

Senator Kennedy interrupts a meeting with his brother-in-law Steve Smith and his executive assistant and speech writer Theodore "Ted" Sorensen to join Jackie and Caroline in the backyard of their home on N Street.

GEORGETOWN. SPRING 1959

many letters he received—correspondence that numbered in the hundreds daily—suggesting responses, doing some research and answering in long hand herself when the correspondent needed a reply in French or Spanish.

She also was very concerned that JFK eat a proper lunch. Before they met, a hot dog or even a candy bar would suffice, but Jackie wanted to make sure he ate healthy and well-balanced meals. She would often bring a basket of food to his office; at other times she would prepare a lunch basket and send it along with George, the longtime family butler. On days when there was no party to attend, they would dine alone at home, Jackie often serving dinner herself and giving the housekeeper the evening off. And Jack liked it that way. He said "I spend my days with politicians—not my nights. I don't want to come home from the Senate and then have to defend my position to my wife all evening." But much of the time there was more work to do after dinner, and Kennedy appreciated his wife's help and advice. Jackie would deal with a briefcase full of correspondence the Senator habitually brought home from the office, and Jack would immerse himself in reading and annotating upcoming senate bills.

In spite of these many activities, most of her day was filled with taking care of, and thoroughly enjoying, Caroline. Motherhood was a natural state for her. Long hours would be spent dressing Caroline and brushing her hair. The nursery sparkled with gay ornaments and cheerful wallpaper. Jackie never seemed to tire of playing games with her daughter or reading her stories. Later, she would say, "If you bungle raising your children, I don't think whatever else you do will matter very much," and finally, in the White House, she said, "I don't want my children to be brought up by nurses and Secret Service men."

This mini merry-go-round, recently installed on the lawn of the Kennedy compound, served as a center of amusement for all the children—Caroline, Bobby Kennedy's eight children, Stevie Smith, Maria and Bobby Shriver, and all their friends. The place absolutely teemed with children, their pets, their nurses and their toys.

HYANNIS PORT, MASSACHUSETTS. SUMMER 1960

On the weekends—if Jack was in town and before their house in Hyannis Port opened for the summer—Jack would often work at home surrounded by close associates such as his executive assistant Ted Sorensen or brother-in-law Steve Smith, who served as a general troubleshooter and was the early coordinator of the still underground but burgeoning Kennedy presidential campaign.

The still vivid memory I have of this week in Georgetown with the Kennedys is Jackie's endless patience—and enthusiasm—in posing for photographs; her ability to sit motionless for portraits, her suggestions for more and different settings or poses, and her total openness, even eagerness, to have Caroline photographed. She would get her daughter ready for the sessions by carefully dressing her without any assistance from the nurse. That attitude and openness, unfortunately, didn't last. By the time Jackie entered the White House, she would "protect" her children from photographers to the point of near paranoia, and this was often in conflict with her husband, who knew and deeply appreciated the fact that his young family was an enormous political asset.

The small antique secretaire in the living room of their home served as Jackie's office, where she answered mail and sent and received invitations.

GEORGETOWN. FALL 1959

39

IV

In the late spring of 1959 I received a call from Steve Smith to come to Washington for the day. I was to meet him at the Esso building, a five-minute walk from the Senate. Once there, I was instructed to follow hand-written and totally obscure signs (the words Kennedy, presidential or campaign were nowhere to be seen) and eventually I arrived in a huge room that looked like a branch of IBM, not a campaign office. Massive computers lined the walls and dozens of technicians were busy feeding and extracting information into and out of these monster machines. Steve explained that this was an information-gathering office, serving to compile the data necessary for a potential Kennedy run for the presidency. He never said that Jack was already running. From time to time, he said, they would need photographs of Kennedy as he was traveling around the country taking the pulse of the people. Was I interested in these occasional trips, and if so what would my charges be? I, of course, was intensely interested and there seemed to be no problem about my charges, but I was unable to get answers to my questions about what I was expected to do. Did they want portraits? Documentary coverage? What was the end use of the pictures? Brochures, magazine pieces, posters?—all the usual questions a photographer asks when being assigned a job. But the only answer was, "You're the artist. You're the photographer. You do what you think is right. We trust you."

That first meeting was in fact prophetic. Until the end of the campaign, it was to be the only instruction I would ever receive except for an occasional request from the candidate such as, "Take a picture of me with these miners and make sure each of them gets a copy, Jacques." Though disconcerting in the beginning, the freedom to cover whatever caught my eye turned out to be a creative boon. I realize now that they knew exactly what they were doing and it had all come down, in its very precision or lack of it, from Bobby and Jack.

During that lovely late summer of 1960, the Kennedy compound was over-run by countless children and pets. Here Jackie enjoys a private moment with Caroline and her dog.

HYANNIS PORT, MASSACHUSETTS. SPRING 1960

I received my first call on a Friday night: Please come to La Guardia Airport, go to the Butler Aviation terminal—the private plane terminal—and ask for the Kennedy plane, which turned out to be a rented turbo-prop. On board were the Senator, Steve Smith, Ted Sorensen and an adviser named Hy Raskin. We flew to Omaha, where Kennedy and a few other non-candidates made an appearance at a Democratic barbecue and fund-raiser. I busily covered everything, and out of that first foray came the later official *JFK for President* poster.

Once back in New York I processed the film, selected a few prints and sent them all off with my invoice. I was paid instantly, but didn't hear anything further about the photographs. As on that first trip to Hyannis Port, I was afraid I had failed again and blamed it on the lack of instructions. But a few weeks later another call came in. This time I was asked to come to California. As the year wore on, and the trips became longer and more frequent, Jackie started to join us as well.

The proper political wife back in the late fifties and early sixties was seen and not heard. It was her job to smile through endless repetitive speeches and never, ever look bored. She was expected to shake hands all day and be terribly interested in whatever the hand shakers had to say. As to food, cold chicken or a barbecue at three different dinner speeches was the norm. In no way did Jackie fit that profile, previously exemplified by Mamie Eisenhower and Bess Truman. Young and vibrant, highly sophisticated, widely traveled, interested in the arts, able to speak several languages and coming from a very privileged background, she hardly fit the mold. And she was frequently regarded with suspicion, especially in the midwest, the far north and the south. She simply wasn't the comfortable, non-threatening maternal figure everybody wanted, nor, for that matter, was Jack the father figure Ike Eisenhower had been. But Jackie was

A brief moment of intimacy as Senator Kennedy pauses in the hallway before leaving for Capitol Hill.

GEORGETOWN. SPRING 1959

43

remarkable, and she became quite accustomed to her assigned role and very skilled in deflecting negative comments from the many kibitzers who invade all early political campaigns. In time she became a real trouper and a valuable asset in her husband's quest for the presidential nomination.

Eventually she would say, "Not many people know how physically wearing such a campaign can be. Some mornings you're up at seven, and you visit a dozen towns during the day. You shake hundreds of hands in the afternoon and hundreds more at night. You get so tired you catch yourself laughing and crying at the same time. But you pace yourself and you get through it. You just look at it as something you have to do."

From the very beginning of the presidential campaign, Kennedy had relied on private planes to get him around the country. First a rented turboprop and later his own Convair, christened *The Caroline*, would transport the candidate, his family and his staff and entourage from meeting to meeting, breakfast to breakfast, speech to speech, an endless round of overlapping and often similar events. Jackie would join the plane in Washington or New York, and while the Senator and his aides would pore over position papers or annotate and correct forthcoming speeches, Jackie would remain her own, private self, completing a needlework rug, crocheting or quilting a spread or wall hanging, studying picture books on art and architecture and reading, always reading, books ranging from Jack Kerouac's *The Beat Generation* to Andre Malraux's *The Voices of Silence*. Whatever political arguments were swirling around, they did not seem to reach or even interest her. She would never involve herself in these discussions, and the occasional commotion didn't distract her either.

But once she reached her destination she would transform herself into the perfect political wife. Starting at the airport all ready to shake hands

On Election Day morning: Shortly after returning from casting their vote in Hyannis Port, the Kennedys posed for me on the lawn of their summer house. JFK was not yet the President, but there was no doubt in his mind that he would be elected. It would take a long day and an anxious night and morning, with his lead diminishing from two million at midnight to barely 100,000 before he would finally be elected.

HYANNIS PORT, MASSACHUSETTS. NOVEMBER 1960

and chat with whatever well-wishers showed up, she would then join the motorcade, paying close attention to every political remark and smiling in agreement to requests for favors such as addressing a group of women who wanted to get the "feminine" view, or autographing notebooks for a class of high school students. She would sit for hours listening to dozens of speeches—including some she had already heard at the previous stop—and try to look alert. This sometimes proved hard to do. When she was asked to speak, especially when a little French or Spanish was called for, she would make a short speech while the Senator stood by grinning proudly. At the end of each dinner or appearance, she would stand bravely in the reception line for up to an hour or more, patiently shaking hands, smiling and signing autographs.

She gave endless interviews to local gossip columnists and woman's page editors who made the most of their opportunity, and the discussion generally focused on homemaking, cooking, child-rearing and other domestic issues. All of the questions were answered, although she had publicly admitted that she wasn't much of a cook and didn't care about the tedium of housekeeping, a frankness that had gotten her into some hot water. She even wrote a weekly column called "Campaign Wife" for Jack's campaign newsletter. And she eventually became adept at jostling her way on to a platform and pushing her way through thousands of screaming, nearly hysterical fans.

These campaign trips were exhausting. They would often start in an eastern state and end up in the far west, all in the same day with dozens of stops in between. A typical day would begin at around 6:30 in the morning with three breakfast speeches known as Kennedy Coffees. From there the caravan would steer toward the airport, making several stops at supermarkets along the way. They'd scramble onto the plane, and the next stop

The Kennedys in the Senator's office on Capitol Hill. Jackie often assisted her husband in his correspondence, dealing mainly with questions from French and Spanish constituents.

WASHINGTON, D.C. FALL 1958

would call for two or three lunch appearances. More supermarket stops would follow. At some, Jackie would address the surprised shoppers over the public address system. The campaign caravan would then proceed to the next town, where several Kennedy Teas would take place. And finally there would be the evening speeches in yet another town. The usual bedtime would be one or two in the morning, often even later.

There were a few times when I saw Jackie visibly upset. Once, after addressing a group of Rotarians dressed as pirates, JFK was required to sign their register in blood—his own blood—which they took from his finger. It was an old tradition, they insisted. Jackie was sickened and unsuccessfully tried to stop it. She turned white, disgusted by the fact that these "traditions" were necessary to get a man elected President.

Quite often, in some small town, Jackie had to face the local aristocracy—generally comprised of middle-aged, apparently Republican women, claiming to be Democrats. Severe looking and critical, they were neither open nor generous. They were there to render judgment on this young woman and considered themselves perfectly fit to do so, demanding answers to questions—political, religious and moral—that Jackie was not always able to answer. Jackie braved these uncomfortable moments, always charming and always seemingly unperturbed, but it took a lot out of her, and it was becoming more and more obvious that politics and the political process was not something she enjoyed.

I grew to believe, in fact, that she began to abhor politics and hated the politicians and the political system many of them stood for, especially those involved in big city and state politics. She was also, by nature, extremely shy and uncomfortable with people not of her sophistication or wide-ranging cultural interests, and found tiresome the endless small

The Kennedys attended church wherever they found themselves on Sunday mornings. Here they are in Oregon on a cold day in 1959 with Jackie already wearing one of her later to become famous pill-box hats. Jack's religion, of course, would soon come under fire, especially in West Virginia and Wisconsin, two crucial primary states. "I wouldn't want Rome to take over this country'" was a far-fetched but very prevalent opinion at the time.

OREGON. WINTER 1959

talk, and at times crude vulgarity and political hypocrisy. Occasionally, she revolted against it by sulking, even disappearing from billed events.

Yet by the time JFK was nominated to be his party's standard-bearer, Jackie had campaigned hard in some sixteen states, from New Hampshire to West Virginia, from Tennessee to California, from New York to Wisconsin, on the way adding Polish and Italian to her vocabulary. She reduced her wardrobe to three basic dresses, a string of pearls and a hat (later, when traveling as the First Lady, her wardrobe would consist of 35 trunks).

She had suffered and absorbed public abuse from Kennedy supporters and opponents alike. Some felt that she was too classy, too different from the average American woman and therefore a detriment to her husband's campaign, and there were printed rumors—surely inspired by the opposition—that Jack and Jackie were about to break up. I can only guess at why she persisted, but I suppose the potential outcome—First Lady of the land—was enough to keep her going.

Jackie and Caroline in the nursery. Jackie was telling her a story about what different people do in a city.

GEORGETOWN. SPRING 1959

51

V

Jackie's last campaign trip took place during the hotly contested West Virginia primary. Jack Kennedy's religion, Catholicism, had become the primary issue in this contest and while it had been an issue as well in the Wisconsin primary, here it became the sole burning issue. Kennedy's very right to serve his country as President had been called into question due to his Catholicism. He was facing violent criticism and his opponents, some invisible and hiding behind the candidacy of Hubert Humphrey, a decent man, united and tried to use the religious issue to defeat him. Even to his own campaign workers, this was the major stumbling block. "There's only one problem. He is a Catholic. That's our God-damned problem," said one of them. Still, he was by now the front runner, having won every single primary contest he had entered.

I had driven to West Virginia in the early days of the primary campaign, and I was to meet the Kennedy staff and entourage at a hotel in Charleston. Upon arrival, I entered a lobby overflowing with a huge mass of humanity. It reminded me of New Year's Eve in Times Square. I found neither Jack nor Bobby nor any of his advisers or staff. But I did find Jackie, sitting near a large table in a black and white large-checked, Chanel-like suit, with a vulgar boutonniere attached to her left lapel. She was staring straight ahead looking almost frightened, while three middle-aged lady volunteers were sipping tea very daintily from bone china cups, watching her suspiciously. There was no eye contact between Jackie and the three, although they sat at the same table. I rescued her, though not before taking a memorable photograph.

By the time of the Democratic Convention in July of 1960, Jackie was well into her pregnancy and she could not and did not attend. She instead stayed with Caroline at the Kennedy compound in Hyannis Port. On the night of the nomination, her mother and stepfather were with her.

During that relatively quiet period in the Kennedy's life before the Senator declared his run for the presidency, Jackie was able to devote much time to decorating the house, to entertaining and to her beloved daughter.

GEORGETOWN. SPRING 1959

According to Jackie, they watched television, her parents relaying the blow-by-blow to her while she painted furiously until five in the morning. Only occasionally would she drop her brushes to watch the action on television herself because she was intent on finishing the painting she was working on that night, and she did. At ten in the morning she gave a press conference. She was now the wife of the democratic presidential candidate and the potential First Lady. The painting that had so occupied her the night before was to be a gift for the Senator's triumphant return from Los Angeles. It depicts a victorious John F. Kennedy returning home from the wars, although she had started the painting long before the convention had chosen JFK and his New Frontier. Her political instincts were obviously intact.

Dressed in Napoleonic garb, the conquering JFK stands in the stern of a small boat named the *Victura II* surrounded by sailors and civilian aides. The boat is approaching its landing quay at the Hyannis Port marina, where it is welcomed by Jackie, Caroline and her nurse Maud Shaw, all waving American flags, the family dog and a brass band with a banner proclaiming *Welcome Back Mr. Jack*. The background shows the Kennedy compound, several boats festooned with flags and fireworks that spell out July 17, 1960. Cats, dogs, neighbors, dozens of servants and Kennedy children, plus a plane with two waving figures, presumably Joe and Rose Kennedy, trailing a banner that says "You've done it again, Johnny, call us at Cap D'Antibes" round out the image. It is a remarkable and extremely complicated painting.

Jackie was a delightful and gifted amateur painter. She worked in a primitive style reminiscent of early American folk art. That same summer, in fact, she produced another watercolor painting as a birthday present for her father-in-law. This one shows the elder Kennedy's Hyannis Port

Senator Kennedy, with Jackie and his aide Dave Powers, accompanied by Congresswoman Edith Green of Oregon, arrives at dusk for a political appearance. Only three supporters came to meet him. It became the future President's favorite picture. "Nobody remembers that today," he exclaimed later, alluding to the fact that they were ignored.

PORTLAND, OREGON. FALL 1959

55

house with the great rolling front lawn opening up to the bottom of the painting. Ambassador Kennedy stands in the lower right wearing summer shorts, Jackie in a bathing suit and carrying diving fins approaches him. Behind her Jack, carrying a golf club, dressed in yellow pants and a red polo shirt, also approaches his father. Caroline in a yellow dress rushes after her father, while nurse Shaw pushing a carriage stands with her arms thrown up in exasperation in the background. The picture is signed *For Grandpa. Love. Jackie. X0.*

The summer of 1960—the time between JFK's nomination and the start of the general election campaign on Labor Day—was to be the last truly uncomplicated time in their lives. Where earlier I had noticed certain strains between them, that was truly a time of togetherness and love. There was a certain amount of innocent clowning and enjoyment of each other. One morning they went swimming in Nantucket Sound and Jack, sitting in a little boat resembling a floating bathtub, was being pushed by Jackie around the bay until the boat overturned, both tumbling into the water and emerging with big grins. What is so remarkable about that water game is the bathing suit and water cap Jackie wore. When you look at these pictures, it's hard to believe that a fashionable woman like Jackie would wear an outfit so reminiscent of the Thirties.

Jack played a lot of golf that summer, and Jackie surrounded herself with many of the Kennedy children. There were picnics on the beach with hot dogs, hamburgers, chips and marshmallows packed into baskets, while Jackie brought her own deviled eggs, salmon and other delicacies.

It's true that there was a clannishness among the Kennedys. They often moved as one and immensely enjoyed one another's company. But Jackie always stayed somewhat apart, even when it came to enjoying these pic-

En route to California from West Virginia, Jackie relaxes with Jack Kerouac's book "The Beat Generation."

ABOARD THE CAROLINE, KENNEDY'S PRIVATE PLANE. SPRING 1960

nics. Although she had rarely joined the rough and tumble family softball games—Kennedys against Visitors—even in the early days of her marriage, her pregnancy kept her from joining any of the numerous softball, football and other rough competitiveness the Kennedys engaged in and cherished. Jack joined her from time to time, fulfilling his own need for privacy while he was with Jackie that summer, and he kept a certain distance from the rest of his family during these few weeks. The two of them were very close, closer than I'd ever seen them, and he genuinely enjoyed Jackie's and Caroline's company. Observing them, I decided that despite the rumors and the recent strains of the election campaign, Jack was genuinely in love with his wife.

But there were more difficult moments as well for Jackie during that blissful summer. Coming down for breakfast one morning, she walked into a front hall flush with friends and total strangers alike. The strangers, a group of ethnic politicians, had just arrived and were conversing in every Eastern language known to man, from Hungarian to Slovak to Russian. Nodding, she entered the sunroom that opened onto the verandah overlooking Nantucket Bay where, much to her surprise, a bunch of Boston Irish politicians—cigars firmly clenched in their mouths and the air stale with smoke—had installed themselves with their wives, waiting for an audience with the Democratic candidate for President. They jumped all over her, clutching at her clothes and grabbing her hand enthusiastically, when all she wanted was to get away and get some breakfast. Finally escaping, she tried the living room where Jack was ensconced with a group of advisers. He impatiently waved his hand when she tried to enter. Now fairly unhappy, she tried the kitchen. But Pierre Salinger, Kennedy's press secretary, was holding a press conference in that room for a large group of reporters. She quietly went

While Senator Kennedy addresses a crowd, Jackie signs autographs for local high-school students.

CALIFORNIA. FALL 1959

59

back upstairs, her privacy violated once again. I felt her unhappiness, her frustration, her anger, and I empathized greatly with her, for I knew this was only the beginning.

Jackie had already lost two babies and was concerned that renewing the strenuous campaign activities after Labor Day might jeopardize her current pregnancy. By now it had become quite clear that she was a tremendous and highly valued campaign asset to her husband, and he wanted her by his side. But she had to make a decision whether to hunker down alone until that fateful election day in November—since every family member and all close and distant friends and acquaintances were to be deeply involved in the campaign—or whether to risk further strain. Jack, she knew, wouldn't be home very much, and she might not see him for two months. It must have been a terribly difficult and lonely time of decision, but she stayed behind, knowing that she could not endure the fifteen-hour-a-day strain.

About the campaign she had said, "We might fly to Oregon for three or four days. Then we would get up at 6:30 and go to breakfasts, luncheons, dinners in different places. Once in Wisconsin we drove fifty miles in below-zero weather and had to leave our car at two or three stops along the way." She remembered those days vividly and knew that the actual campaign would be even more stressful, and she didn't feel that she could go through it again. JFK, of course, had a different, much happier memory of those primary days. He told the press that Caroline's first words were "plane, goodbye and New Hampshire, and she recently learned to say Wisconsin and West Virginia. Any day now she is expected to come out with Maryland and Oregon." I wasn't exactly looking forward to the stress of the campaign either, because I knew that nothing would stop the candidate from reaching a speaking engagement or campaign stop, cer-

The role of political wives during the Fifties and Sixties was to sit by and wait while their husbands made their speeches, smiling and looking happy when called upon. Jackie wasn't spared that fate.

CALIFORNIA, SPRING 1960

tainly not such minor inconveniences as intolerable flying conditions. I remembered quite a few of the bumpy plane rides that brought me very close to God and gave me instant religion.

The general election campaign began in Detroit on Labor Day. By this time the Kennedys had achieved national icon status, and the crowds appearing at every stop, led by noisy and enthusiastic young women, became larger and larger until the candidate was literally mobbed and torn apart by his supporters. Jackie followed the campaign on television and waited for the daily call from the Senator. She also gave some interviews and contributed articles and ideas to the campaign literature. And in spite of her changed feelings toward the general press, she did make herself available for some interviews and to me, for photography. Twice that fall I left the campaign to photograph her for a number of magazine covers, and she joined the campaign on a few occasions to attend a political dinner or address a French or Spanish-speaking crowd.

In the early part of the campaign, on a Sunday morning after mass, the Kennedys quietly slipped into the local diner for breakfast. Nobody recognized them, and they sat undisturbed. Six months later neither Jackie nor her husband would be able to enjoy that kind of privacy ever again.

A SMALL TOWN IN OREGON. LATE FALL 1959

VI

By the start of the general election campaign however, Jackie's outlook and attitude had changed considerably. Before, she had been outgoing and willing to let the public and press into her private life in order to help the campaign. Now, she had become frightened by the aggressive and intrusive press demanding ever more personal details about her life, questions she felt she simply could not respond to. In addition, she was concerned about the security of not only her husband, but Caroline as well. There had been rumors of kidnappings and death threats and, while many were unsubstantiated, they had to be taken seriously.

She was fatigued and worried about her health and felt that she couldn't really make much of a contribution. It was now up to Jack and Lyndon Johnson to carry the rest of the campaign. She had done her part, and going out there would again expose her to the press. But the pressure to campaign, even from her husband, was enormous. After all, Pat Nixon walked in close step with her husband and Lady Bird was an inveterate campaigner. Jackie was torn, but she had decided it would be too much, that she would remain at home for much of the campaign. It meant that she probably wouldn't see her husband much.

Although she was no longer present on the campaign trail, Jackie's voice was very much heard. And it was a far different voice from the one I had heard before. Suddenly there were conflicts, especially during the few occasions when the Senator came back to Hyannis Port, where she stayed for most of the rest of the campaign.

Jackie had asked to see some of the photos I had taken during the summer. She had shown *Vogue* magazine a series of my prints and they wanted to publish them. At the same time *Modern Screen*, an unlikely medium for a political family profile, also wanted to run the pictures. *Vogue*, of

Jackie brushes Caroline's hair in the foyer of their Georgetown townhouse.

GEORGETOWN. EARLY FALL 1959

course, wouldn't touch the pictures if they also ran in *Modern Screen,* even some from the same session. I would have much preferred a spread in *Vogue* to one in *Modern Screen.*

The problem was that *Vogue* had a circulation of 300,000 and *Modern Screen's* was roughly four million. Moreover, the latter magazine's circulation profile fit the profile of the typical Democratic and thereby Kennedy voter much more closely—blue-collar and middle-class women age 18 to 40—whereas *Vogue's* profile was upper-class Republican. I couldn't give the photographs to both magazines, and I didn't dare make the decision myself, so I left the decision up to the candidate. The answer was unequivocal: *Modern Screen.* "There isn't a single vote for me among all these stuffy society dames," he said. I had no choice but to comply with JFK's wishes. Jackie was furious. She felt I had betrayed her, and although I tried to explain my obligations to the candidate and the campaign and offered her other, equally fine photographs, she refused to consider them. Much to my distress, I don't think she ever really forgave me. It was not to be our first such conflict.

As the general campaign got under way, my assignment gradually changed. Where up to this point I had been hired on an irregular, unofficial basis, the assignment now escalated into more and more days per week until it became a full-time, 18-hour-a-day, seven-day-a-week occupation. I had a very successful studio in New York and had to decide to either stay with the campaign and dump all my other clients, or quit the campaign. It was a difficult decision, for while I loved and admired JFK and had developed a great chemistry with him and a deep friendship with Bobby, it was far from certain that he would win the election. Moreover, I was much too innocent, even ignorant, to contemplate what victory would mean. But I was cognizant of the history-

The candidate's wife is being assessed by the local aristocracy at a Democratic rally.

WEST VIRGINIA. SUMMER 1960

67

in-the-making that I was a part of, and the campaign was an ever-changing, exhilarating daily blast, a happening. It was a once-in-a-lifetime photographic opportunity. I opted to stay. And one day, as I bounded up the stairs of the campaign plane, someone pinned an *Official* badge on me. Although I hadn't asked for the honor, I was now the official campaign photographer. And instantly I began to get deluged daily for photographs—by newspapers and magazines, domestic and foreign, TV stations, local and state Democratic committees—until I finally brought along a portable darkroom, developing the day's shoot and sending out prints on a regular basis.

The remarkable thing about that segment of the campaign is that no one outside of Jackie ever asked to see my daily takes. If JFK or Bobby or other members of the campaign staff saw and liked some of my published work, they would congratulate me, but everybody was so busy, so totally involved with their own tasks, that they didn't have time to question me about what I was doing. "Getting any good shots, Jacques?" was the most the candidate would ever ask, although he did have a remarkable memory about specific photographs he had asked me to send to various supporters. Weeks after a session he would ask whether I had sent pictures to a group of miners or political insiders he had promised photographs to. Amazing!

Jackie was particularly concerned about the Nixon–Kennedy debates. During the fourth debate in New York on October 21, 1960, ABC had thoughtfully provided Bobby with a private suite that overlooked the debating platform, and Jackie had come up to join him. Sitting there with Bobby, her sister Lee Radziwill and campaign aide Kenny O'Donnell (later to become the President's appointments secretary), she watched the debate on foreign policy wearing a short-sleeved black dress with a brooch her only jewelry, looking quite haggard, very worried and very

Senator Kennedy and Jackie in a receiving line to meet the locals and sign autographs.

CALIFORNIA. SPRING 1960

69

pregnant. She had watched the earlier debates on television, but she felt the need to experience this last one close up. But these appearances were difficult for her because ever since JFK had "won" the first debate, the crush of people had become unbearable.

Later in the campaign, after Jack won the New York primary, she joined him in a ticker-tape parade up Broadway. Riding in an open car with thousands of New Yorkers expressing their joy and admiration for this magical couple, she looked radiant and happy. In a way, that parade was the climax of Jackie's involvement in the Kennedy campaign.

The Kennedys recite the Pledge of Allegiance prior to addressing the audience at a California High School.

CALIFORNIA. SPRING 1960

VII

On November 8, 1960 Senator and Mrs. Kennedy showed up at the West End Library in Boston to cast their votes. Jackie later claimed that she cast only one vote, JFK for President. "It is a rare thing to be able to vote for one's husband for President of the United States," she said. In fact, because of her pregnancy, she had voted by absentee ballot. Showing up at the polls was a political gesture. Then, back in Hyannis Port, she went into seclusion.

The Kennedys had set up their command center in Bobby's house, barely a hundred feet from Jack and Jackie's home. There, a battery of telephones connected them with key precincts around the country and reports came in on a regular basis. Every living relative, staff member, friend and hanger-on joined in a cacophony of confusion. The early news was good—Jack was two million votes ahead—and there was much jubilation. But as the evening wore on and results came in from the midwest and far west, the huge lead started to diminish. At one point, in fact, NBC's computer declared Nixon the winner, but shortly thereafter their commentator negated the report. By 3:00 A.M. JFK's lead had shrunk to a mere 200,000 votes and the candidate, who had joined the faithful at Bobby's house for a short visit, declared that there was little he could do and he went to sleep. Gutsy, I thought. The rest of us remained, and I don't know when I finally went to sleep on a cot in the maids' quarters. I was told that Jackie spent much of her time that evening sifting through a stack of photographs I had given her of the entire campaign.

I woke up at 7:00 the next morning only to find that the entire family, excluding JFK and Jackie, had already left for a walk on the beach. I joined them, and then the now worried and concerned family and friends reassembled in Bobby's house. We were soon joined by JFK and his father, who had also gone to sleep early the previous night. There were

Senator and Mrs. Kennedy: a political team in action. This was before Jackie's pregnancy prevented her further campaigning.

WASHINGTON STATE. SPRING 1960

endless conferences upstairs in the children's rooms, downstairs in the living and dining rooms, around the stairways and out on the sun porch. The mood was palpably strained. Eventually everyone gathered around the television set, grimly watching the still indecisive returns. JFK, clutching a pencil tightly in his hand and stabbing it into his thigh from time to time, finally crushed it absentmindedly into pieces. Jackie was nowhere to be seen.

It wasn't until 11:00 A.M. that Mayor Richard Daley of Chicago appeared on national television and, pulling a sheet of paper out of his back pocket, announced that John F. Kennedy had triumphed in the state of Illinois. Kennedy had been only eleven electoral votes short of the 269 needed to win, and Illinois put him over the top (those votes would later be challenged by the Nixon campaign, but irregularities in neighboring Lafayette County in favor of the Republicans squelched the challenge). It was all over. John F. Kennedy would be the 35th President of the United States.

It was an awesome realization for me, as it was for the rest of the family and friends present. JFK, Bobby, Ethel, Eunice, all were gathered on the sun porch looking admiringly at their brother. He was now Mr. President, even to his family. The next stop was the Hyannis Armory, where the world's press was waiting.

Before everyone was to take off for the press conference, I knew I had a job to do. This would most likely be the last time that the entire family would be gathered in one small space. Once JFK reached the White House that would never happen again. I realized that a historic photograph was waiting to be taken—the entire Kennedy Clan, parents, children and in-laws, at the very moment of their triumph. I brought the matter up to JFK, who agreed, as did Bobby, but they left it up to me to

While the Senator addresses a nearly empty Union Hall of longshoremen, who seem unimpressed, Jackie chats with one of the members. She too is all but ignored.

COOS BAY, OREGON. FALL 1959

assemble all the others. Excited, almost delirious, a family picture was the last thing on their minds. Tomorrow. Later. But I knew there would never be a tomorrow. In desperation, I finally appealed to Joe Kennedy, the patriarch and my first sponsor. He agreed and announced that the photograph would be taken prior to leaving for the Armory.

But as I tried to arrange the photo, I spotted Jackie just outside the library window. She seemed to be in a state of shock. She hadn't entered Bobby's house where everybody had watched TV or her father–in–law's house where everyone was now gathering for the picture, and she wasn't participating in the mood of celebration and happy camaraderie. Instead she had thrown a raincoat over her shoulders—there was a slight drizzle coming down—and gone out for a walk along the sea. Although, like every family and staff member, Jackie had anticipated this moment for a long time, she seemed stunned by the realization that she was now the First Lady. As I watched with some fascination, I saw a reporter rush up to her with outstretched hand in congratulation. She took the hand but instantly walked on. Nobody else noticed or paid any attention to her. Everyone was too preoccupied and overwhelmed by this triumph after the three long years of reaching for it.

Frantically, I tried to get everyone into the library. While some family members drifted in, others, getting bored, drifted out again. Finally, all were gathered except Jackie. Where was she? I told the President–elect that I had seen her walking down to the beach. He went out to get her, but he came back alone. She was getting dressed, he said, and everyone waited. She finally appeared, looking radiant and quite beautiful. And whatever it was that drove her down to the beach to commune with the sea had been resolved. JFK walked over to the door and took her by the arm, and the entire family rose to applaud her. It was a magnificent moment.

The Senator and Mrs. Kennedy leave an Elks meeting in California.

CALIFORNIA. SPRING 1960

77

The world's press, gathered at the Hyannis Armory, greeted the young President-elect and his very pregnant wife with uncritical admiration. The seasoned reporters present behaved as though this was their own victory as well as Kennedy's. It was to be the beginning of an unusual bond between a President and the press, a love affair that ignored many presidential peccadilloes that would cripple later candidates. It also was the beginning of a stand-off between the First Lady and, in Jackie's mind, a manipulative press. They would become very distrustful and suspicious of each other. But this was a day of celebration. Kennedy's speech to the press and the world at that gathering was well short of major policy pronouncements. Instead he intoned, with his extended family gathered behind him, "So now my wife and I prepare for a new administration and for a new baby. Thank you!"

The time between the end of the Democratic Convention and the start of the general election campaign was the last true carefree and private time the Kennedys were to have. They enjoyed themselves enormously, the Senator sailing and playing golf, Jackie arranging picnics and spending time with all the children at the Kennedy compound.

HYANNIS PORT, MASSACHUSETTS. AUGUST 1960

VIII

Camelot started rather inauspiciously, in a blizzard. On Thursday afternoon, January 19, 1961, an unexpected storm dumped eight inches of snow on Washington D.C., paralyzing the city as it was preparing for the inauguration of the 35th President of the United States. Under the direction of Frank Sinatra, the Kennedy people had put together a glamorous Inaugural Gala the night before the swearing–in ceremony at Washington's National Guard Armory. It was unprecedented. The Gala had been billed as the greatest inaugural show ever presented, and it featured such stars as Nat "King" Cole, Ella Fitzgerald, Gene Kelly, Ethel Merman, Harry Belafonte, Fredric March, Laurence Olivier, Tony Curtis, Janet Leigh and Leonard Bernstein, among others. Even the audience was going to be packed with Hollywood and Broadway luminaries. And of course the Kennedys were going to be the stars of stars.

The trouble was "nothing in Washington moved." I was dressed in casual slacks and sports jacket, ignoring the official black-tie invitation. I just needed to get to the Armory, formally or informally dressed, along with an enormous crowd, equally eager and irrepressible in their desire to celebrate. I arrived at the half-empty Armory nearly two hours late, and made my way up to the presidential box, where the President-elect and his wife finally appeared at 11:00 P.M., he in a tuxedo, Jackie in a truly regal ankle length, slim dress of white silk ottoman adorned with a rosette at the waistline, quarter-length sleeves and long white gloves. Carrying a small white purse, she wore an emerald and diamond necklace and matching earrings that accented the simple round collar of her dress. The couple arrived with Frank Sinatra at their side. By then the hall had filled up and the entire crowd, accustomed to the Mamie Eisenhower and Bess Truman years, let out a gasp of astonishment and delight as she entered the box. The President was in a high and boisterous mood. He

Jackie and Caroline continue their games on the porch of the Kennedy summer home after the Senator left for a golf game. "I Can Fly" was Caroline's favorite book then.

HYANNIS PORT, MASSACHUSETTS. AUGUST 1960

kept disappearing from his official box, greeting friends here and there, bobbing up in unexpected places all night long. He was obviously having the time of his life. His Secret Service detail however, used to the bureaucratic discipline of the Eisenhower years, was in a state of shock as they got their first taste of what it would be like to deal with this president. They kept losing him and for some reason thought I was hiding him. "No," I protested over and over again, "I don't know where he is."

Jackie remained in her box, watching and applauding the entertainment, but she seemed even more amused by the audience, all of whom were in a state of near hysterical exhilaration. After all, the Democrats had been out of power for eight years and this was their time to celebrate. Jackie left shortly after the show, but JFK, one day away from being sworn in, stayed to the bitter end.

The gala performance was presented with gusto by the assemblage of stars and was a great success, but the true stars of the evening were the President-elect and his wife, Jacqueline. The myth that came to be known as Camelot had begun.

A great part of the carefree days between the convention and the start of the general election campaign were spent in the water.

HYANNIS PORT, MASSACHUSETTS. AUGUST 1960

IX

January 20, 1961, Inauguration Day, was bitterly cold. Although the blizzard had stopped during the night, the temperature was in the low twenties and a bitter wind was howling through the town. The streets were piled high with huge mounds of snow. The Kennedy administration was about to begin.

I had reached N Street at about 9:00, groggy but alert after the Gala, and shortly after 11:00 A.M. the Speaker of the House, Sam Rayburn, arrived to accompany Senator and Mrs. Kennedy to the White House, where they would pick up President Eisenhower, as protocol demanded, and drive with him to the Capitol for the swearing in. The President-elect, wearing a morning coat and carrying a silk hat, looked splendid. Jackie, who wore a light beige wool coat with three large buttons down the center and a matching pill-box hat—a hat style later to become famous— looked like a happy young girl off to a party. The bubble-top car they entered bore the presidential seal.

At the White House, the outgoing President invited his successor inside for a chat and soon Jack Kennedy and Ike Eisenhower, Jackie and Mamie and finally Lyndon Johnson and Richard Nixon came down the steps to drive—each group in a separate car—to the inaugural stand for the swearing in of the new president.

But first Marian Anderson, the great African American opera singer, sang the "Star Spangled Banner," and Robert Frost, the ancient yankee poet, tried to recite a poem he had especially written for the occasion. He had to abandon his attempt in the glaring sun, and instead recited the new President's favorite poem, the most famous line being, "I have many promises to keep, and miles to go before I sleep." It was a verse that JFK the campaigner had repeated over and over on his campaign stops.

On a Sunday after church, the Kennedys romp in Nantucket Bay in front of their house in a plastic boat hardly larger than a bathtub. Their enjoyment is obvious.

HYANNIS PORT, MASSACHUSETTS, AUGUST 1960

Finally, after his swearing in, the President proclaimed in his speech, "Ask not what your country can do for you, but what you can do for your country," and he added, "In the long history of the world, only a few generations have been granted the role of defending freedom in its hour of maximum danger," a reference to the still raging Cold War. He continued, "I do not believe that any of us would exchange places with any other people or any other generation. The energy, the faith, the devotion which we bring to this endeavor will light our country and all who serve it, and the glow from that fire will truly light the world." His speech inspired and energized the nation—and the world.

Jackie herself, seated between Pat Nixon and Lady Bird Johnson—two future first ladies—her hands in a muff to protect her from the bitter cold, had listened quietly and with dignity to this clarion call, and now she and her husband presented themselves for the first time as President and First Lady at a luncheon at the old Supreme Court chamber, where former president Harry Truman, Chief Justice Warren and endless well-wishers paid their respects to the handsome young couple.

Later, on their drive up Pennsylvania Avenue to the White House in their open car—eerily similar to the tragic events in Dallas less than three years later—they joked as I ran along to catch the moment. "You should have run for President, not photographer," Kennedy yelled out, "it's more comfortable." Arriving at the White House to review the Inaugural Parade, an endless spectacle that lasted for hours, Jackie spent about an hour on the reviewing stand in the bitter cold, then left to get ready for the Inaugural Balls that night. She had already made her mark.

There were five Balls that night at different locations. Jackie managed to attend three of them. The new President attended all five. Jackie's dress that night, again white, was equally stunning but a clear contrast to the

A giggling Jackie in a rare moment of total relaxation looks absolutely ravishing in a bathing cap and suit—swimwear that is now back in style.

HYANNIS PORT, MASSACHUSETTS. AUGUST 1960

one she had shown off the night before at the Gala. This time she wore no jewelry except for a pair of diamond pendant earrings. The dress itself, actually an underdress, was a slim sheath of silk chiffon starting from the ankles and ending at the hips, where the material was transformed to near shoulder height by a magnificent melange of silver embroidery. A sleeveless chiffon veil worn over the embroidery completed the design. Shoulder-length white kid gloves completed the ensemble. She carried the same white silk purse she had carried the day before. When she entered her balcony seat with the President, dressed in tails beside her, the audience, assembled on the ballroom floor thirty feet below, again gasped its approval and astonishment. The President, in his short speech, addressed himself to the absurdity of the occasion. "I think this is an ideal way to spend an evening," he said, "you looking up at us and we looking down at you."

From that day forward, Jackie was truly the First Lady of the land, a term she hated but could not shake. She would be imitated in everything she did—her hair styles, her hats, her clothes. There would be Jackie look–alike contests, and her every movement was recorded by the White House and the world's press, especially by the lady reporters who worked for the nation's women's pages and women's magazines—until it would become a real burden to her when yet another interviewer would ask her the very questions she considered to be intrusive, questions no one had ever thought of asking Bess Truman or Mamie Eisenhower. Americans, in their adoration, had begun to think that they owned her.

Jackie was an enthusiastic amateur artist who painted in a primitive Grandma Moses style, and some of her paintings are enchanting. Her gift to JFK on his return from the Democratic Convention was a painting depicting him as "Washington Crossing the Delaware," but wearing a Napoleonic tunic.

HYANNIS PORT, MASSACHUSETTS. SEPTEMBER 1960

X

The morning after the last Inaugural Ball ended, I met the new President and accompanied him to the Oval Office. It is a moment I will never forget. The room had been cleared of his predecessor's mementos and the walls were painted a drab green interrupted only by blank spaces where pictures had hung. But most remarkable was the inlaid parquet floor, a craftsman's dream. It was indented with hundreds of little holes, cleat marks left by Eisenhower's golf shoes. The old warrior had practiced his golf swing there.

The Kennedys on Election Day, November 8, 1960.

Within a few short weeks, Jackie's invisible hand had transformed that beautiful and historic room. She had found an old desk in the White House basement made from the timber of the *HMS Resolute*, a gift from Queen Victoria in 1878 to President Rutherford B. Hayes. Aware of her husband's love of the sea, Jackie had the old desk restored to its former splendor, and JFK loved it. The walls were repainted in a soft off-white, and it was to eventually become a very personal room, replete with pictures of sailing ships and bound volumes of the President's heroes, including Thomas Jefferson, Abraham Lincoln and Franklin Roosevelt, and the poetry of Robert Frost. Transforming that room was the beginning of Jackie's intensive and successful effort to restore the White House—perhaps the world's most famous building—to its rightful glory as a place of reverence and a historic museum dedicated to the American people.

My assignment completed, I wanted to return to New York to reopen my studio, but the President asked me to stay. "Stick around, Jacques, and I'll make it worth your while." He kept his word. But while the opportunity, the chance, the luck, for a young photographer to freely roam the White House was an overwhelming, near spiritual experience, it also intensified my earlier conflicts with Jackie.

Jackie, by the time we reached the White House, had become totally wary of the press, and especially of photographers. And for good reason. In the

HYANNIS PORT, MASSACHUSETTS. NOVEMBER 8, 1960

hospital for John Jr.'s birth, three weeks after the election, a photographer in a white gown had jumped out of a closet as she was being wheeled to the delivery room. Rumors of kidnapping threats and even assassination plots had multiplied, and loiterers had been apprehended near the White House on several occasions. She was growing increasingly concerned about her children's privacy and well being, and insisted that they grow up in as normal a way as possible. Where just a few months earlier she had been most comfortable with cameras, even delighted at being photographed, she now became harder and harder to reach.

In any case the appreciation and understanding of my work on the part of the President was quite different from that of the First Lady. Jack Kennedy had always looked at me and my work as reportage, excellent photojournalism to be sure, but the result was meant to be a document, a moment captured for posterity. I'm sure it's for that reason that he asked me to stay on. He wanted his administration documented by someone he trusted to get it right, by someone who didn't miss anything. For Jackie, however, photography was art. She looked at a photograph and saw composition and the qualities of light and shadow. She was the more creative of the two and appreciated my work for its artistic value. But in the process she dismissed the documentary side of my work, and that is why the conflict between us became serious, because I was a photographer, both artistic *and* journalistic.

Halfway through the first year of the administration, the President asked me to take some photographs of Caroline roaming the White House and let Ben Bradlee, then the Washington bureau chief of *Newsweek*, publish the pictures. I told him I couldn't do it. "Why not?" he asked innocently, knowing full well the reason. "Because Jackie won't allow it," I said. "Don't tell her," he said. "Mr. President, I can hardly take pictures of

John F. Kennedy was elected President of the United States shortly after 11:30 A.M. on Wednesday, November 9, 1960, the day after Election Day, by a narrow 100,000 votes. The world's press was now waiting for the President-elect at the Hyannis Port Armory. I realized this would be the only chance I would ever get to photograph the entire Kennedy clan. They would never again be together in one small place like this.

HYANNIS PORT, MASSACHUSETTS. NOVEMBER 1960

Caroline, have them published in *Newsweek*, and not have Jackie find out who took the pictures, even if I use a pseudonym or reject a credit line." "Don't worry," he said with a mischievous smile, "I'll straighten it out, but Ben really needs the pictures." So I did what the leader of the free world told me to do, and although my relationship with Jackie continued to be cordial, and I did continue to cover her—especially on trips abroad—the bond had been broken. I have always regretted that, but I had no choice, and of course I could never explain it even if the opportunity arose. As for the President, I doubt that he ever admitted his role in the plot.

But the occasional difficulty notwithstanding, those early years in the White House were an exhilarating and unforgettable experience. The young President—informal, witty, spontaneous and full of fun—made even tense days seem joyful. The ponderous atmosphere pervading the White House under the Eisenhower administration, with its endless cabinet meetings and solemn, humorless, business-oriented pronouncements and press conferences, was being replaced with a lighthearted approach to most issues, at least as far as the public was concerned. During the campaign he had said that the presidency would not be easy in the 1960s, and now the President had admitted to the press that no man could realize until reaching the office how heavy that burden would be. But Kennedy's frequent press conferences, although often dealing with serious and frightening issues, became known for their humor and were turned into national events, with the President answering silly questions from grandstanding journalists with witty, quick-on-the-draw punchlines that had the entire country chuckling.

Jackie's contributions were on the cultural and intellectual level. She appointed a Fine Arts Committee to help locate relevant antique furniture and raise funds to purchase items that would restore the White House to its original splendor. She redecorated the private quarters of

President-elect and Mrs. Kennedy, on their way to the Inauguration, leave their Georgetown house for the last time. That day they will move into the White House.

GEORGETOWN. JANUARY 20, 1961

95

the First Family, installing a family kitchen, a pantry and a large dining room so that food no longer had to be brought up from two floors below. She also retained a French chef and charged him with improving the food served at official White House functions. And most important, she transformed these White House dinners into major social events. No longer were the guests a collection of wealthy businessmen. Now, attendees were members of the world's intellectual and artistic elite, including Pablo Casals, Igor Stravinsky, Leonard Bernstein, Rudolf Nureyev and Margot Fonteyn, Andre Malraux and an assemblage of American Nobel Prize-winners. They in turn often rubbed shoulders with the stars of stage and screen and popular music. JFK, in addressing the Nobel laureates, began his welcoming speech with the words, "I think this is the most extraordinary collection of talent, of human knowledge, that has ever been gathered together at the White House, with the possible exception of when Thomas Jefferson dined alone." Jack and Jackie were becoming a fun couple, amply supported by all the other Kennedys.

While improving the White House decor and gourmet cooking and the level of guests, Jackie never neglected her children. A playground, complete with a tree house, was built on the south lawn. A special school was set up on the third floor for Caroline and a group of her friends. And a menagerie was added. Caroline's famous pony was eventually joined by a pet canary, a gray cat, a Welsh terrier, thirteen ducks, two hamsters, and Pushinka, a white puppy sent by Nikita Khrushchev.

Jackie's Fine Arts Committee was also a great success. Within a few months they unearthed furniture belonging to George Washington, Abraham Lincoln, Ulysses Grant, James Madison, James Monroe, Martin van Buren and others. And, in February of 1962, when she led the entire country on a tour of the White House via television, millions

Following JFK's by now historic inaugural speech, the crowd, including President Eisenhower, Vice Presidents Nixon and Johnson, the entire Senate and House, the Supreme Court and other dignitaries, left the inaugural platform. Somehow Jackie, wearing a white pill-box hat and white coat stands out from the large crowd mostly dressed in black.

THE CAPITOL. JANUARY 20, 1961

of viewers tuned in to the show. By then the annual number of visitors to the White House had risen to over 1,500,000 people, all curious about what the First Lady was up to.

And of course Jackie became an international symbol of elegance and style. The clothes she wore were duplicated and on the rack within weeks of her first appearance in them. The pillbox hat became a national obsession. The designers who made her clothes became rich and famous, as did her hairdressers, and everyone else even slightly connected to her looks or style. Even Maud Shaw, the children's nanny, would eventually write a best-selling book. JFK accepted all this with a certain amused detachment, but Jackie had a more difficult time with this kind of adoration. It could, at times, become stifling.

Both Kennedys, moreover, were aware of their real power in spite of the sometimes lighthearted and self-deprecating approach they took. For me, adjusting to this whirlwind was sometimes complicated. I remember working late one night alone with the President in the Oval Office. He was speaking into a Dictaphone, occasionally picking up the telephone and annotating letters. I was taking pictures. It was late, perhaps 11:00 P.M., and the President asked me to find out about an issue at hand. I have by now forgotten the specifics, but I well remember the occasion. I went to the door, stopped and turned toward JFK. "How do I do this, Mr. President?" "Just stick your head out the door and whisper, Jacques." It worked, and it was my first lesson in power, which I learned to apply myself as I moved through the power structure of the Kennedy White House.

President and First Lady Jacqueline Kennedy wind their way up Pennsylvania Avenue from the Capitol to the White House, where they will watch the Inaugural Parade. The open car is an eerie reminder of the later, tragic events.

THE CAPITOL. JANUARY 20, 1961

XI

In the late Spring of 1961 President and Mrs. Kennedy took their first trip abroad. They were to go to Paris, Vienna and London. In Paris they were to meet General Charles de Gaulle, a man both President Kennedy and Jackie greatly admired, and in Vienna the President was to confront Nikita Khrushchev, the belligerent chairman of the Soviet Union, who had caused such terrible problems for President Eisenhower. It was a meeting JFK wasn't looking forward to. But London was to be a mostly private visit, where the President would become the godfather to his sister-in-law Lee Radziwill's newborn child. Kennedy had also arranged several meetings with Prime Minister Harold Macmillan, a statesman whose advice he trusted and whom he respected greatly. The Kennedys had also been invited to dine with Queen Elizabeth at Buckingham Palace, a nostalgic event for this President, whose father had been the American ambassador to the United Kingdom during a time when the young man had met the Queen's parents.

It was to be a tumultuous trip with the world's press in attendance every step of the way. Mrs. Kennedy asked me to come along since the President wanted the christening recorded, but she wanted it kept strictly private. No press was to be admitted. I acceded happily, not knowing what I was getting into.

Because of the huge number of press and television personnel—as well as government leaders and White House staff—accompanying the first couple to Europe, a special plane had been chartered, and even heavyweight newsmen and friends of the President were assigned to that plane as was I, frustrating my desire to ride in Air Force One. But our arrival in Paris proved to be worth that slight disappointment.

Paris went wild over the arrival of the Kennedys. That sophisticated and often cynical city gave the President and his lady a tumultuous welcome,

Jacqueline Kennedy appears for the first time as First Lady of the land at the Inaugural Ball on January 20, 1961. Jackie is wearing a slender, tube-like white chiffon and satin gown, arm-length white gloves and surprisingly little jewelry.

Although John F. Kennedy was the 35th President of the United States, Jackie was the 31st First Lady.

THE ARMORY, WASHINGTON, D.C. JANUARY 20, 1961

and over a million Parisians lined the sidewalks simply to catch a glimpse as the Kennedy entourage drove in from the airport.

Kennedy, in response, said what a great honor it was to be received with such enthusiasm and he told his first Parisian press conference that "I do not think it altogether inappropriate to introduce myself to the audience. I am the man who accompanied Jacqueline Kennedy to Paris, and I have enjoyed it."

Indeed, Jackie was an instant hit, adored at every appearance she made. And as a former student at Paris' Sorbonne, the word went out that she was "back in town." She visited a child care center and a museum, attended many receptions and of course the official dinners at the Elysée Palace and at Versailles. Her every appearance became a phenomenon. General de Gaulle, normally an unbending figure, was at his most gallant, since he could converse with Jackie in his own language. All of this aided the President, who needed the respect of this French authoritarian and his appraisal on how to approach Khrushchev in Vienna.

But for a mere presidential photographer, life wasn't quite so easy. I was lodged at the Hotel Crillon—one of Paris' finest hotels—next to the American embassy at the Place de la Concorde. The first event was to be an evening reception at the Elysée Palace, the official residence and office of French presidents, the equivalent of the White House. The party was the most sought-after ticket in town, with anyone worth his reputation needing to be seen there. Kennedy, of course, wanted it covered, but "Le Grand Charlie," as he was known in France, hated photographers, regarding them as equal to household pests. So a battle ensued between the visiting President and the resident potentate on whether the party would be covered, and who would cover it. Obviously, I was first in line

Jackie, wearing a glittering gown and a dazzling smile, waits to enter the presidential box at the Inaugural Ball.

THE ARMORY, WASHINGTON, D.C. JANUARY 20, 1961

on the American side, but the DeGaulle press office continued to give confusing information via our own Pierre Salinger as to who was allowed and how to proceed. One ploy they used was to change the dress code, switching from tuxedos to tails and back to tuxedos for the "photographers." There finally were to be three, individually representing the United States, Europe and the White House. Finally, on a Friday night, the decisive word arrived: it was to be tails. I had packed a tuxedo in anticipation of the events. I didn't even own tails. But the concierge at the Crillon—God bless all the great concierges of this world—came through. He produced beautiful tails on a Saturday. They even fit, more or less.

The party, billed as a formal dinner but served buffet style, was magnificent, and Jackie was the undisputed star. Surrounded by elegant Parisians, all outfitted in the most stylish clothes by the finest French designers, she outshone them all, looking stunning in a sleeveless white silk dress with an intricate weave design and a scalloped top, long white gloves reaching almost to her shoulders, her hair in a chic bun and only one piece of jewelry, a pair of diamond earrings. She was the envy of every woman there and the pride of the President and the American delegation.

The following evening was to be an even more opulent affair. President de Gaulle had thrown open the palace of Versailles, playground of the Sun King Louis XIV, where the Kennedys were the guests of honor at a glittering sit-down dinner affair complete with a performance by the Paris ballet company. Again, the reception for the young President and his First Lady could only be described as dazzling. The trip, of course, was not all festive. The President addressed NATO and SHAPE, gave his first widely distributed overseas press conference and huddled for hours with General de Gaulle in preparation for his forthcoming meeting with

The First Lady in the presidential box during the Inaugural Ball.

WASHINGTON, D.C. JANUARY 20, 1961

chairman Khrushchev. Jackie, meanwhile, often accompanied by Madame de Gaulle, concentrated on spreading good will among the people of Paris. And then it was on to Vienna.

The President was well prepared for his meeting with the Russian leader. De Gaulle had warned him that Khrushchev would attempt to threaten him with cutting off the Berlin corridor and the seizure of West Berlin, but that he would be bluffing. Kennedy was steeled for that confrontation but nevertheless shaken by Khrushchev's bullying vehemence and threats. But the Soviet leader greatly underestimated his opponent, and Kennedy remained calm, taking the Soviet leader's measure carefully, something that would help him later in the Cuban Missile Crisis confrontation. Asking about the singular medal Khrushchev was wearing, he was told it was the Lenin Peace Prize. "I hope you get to keep it," Kennedy told Khrushchev. But while the two men were locked in a bitter confrontational battle, Khrushchev adored Jackie instantly.

The Austrian chancellor hosted a reception at Schloss Schoenbrunn, the beautiful rococo castle in Vienna, to which he invited both the American and the Soviet delegations. It too featured a ballet performance. Upon his arrival, Khrushchev was asked whether he would pose for a picture shaking hands with Kennedy. Taking one look at Jackie, he replied that he would rather shake hands with her, which he promptly proceeded to do. They then were seated next to each other and Khrushchev, his eyes bulging, could hardly contain himself. Jackie, once again looking demure but devastating in a white silk sleeveless dress with a round collar, long white gloves and a bow at her hips, her hair in an intricate coif, responded readily to the chairman's attention and soon they were laughing and bantering back and forth. It was a different Khrushchev from the one we had seen earlier.

Jacqueline Kennedy was happiest when playing or reading to her children. She was a devoted mother. Here she is with Caroline in the summer of 1961.

HYANNIS PORT, MASSACHUSETTS. SUMMER 1961

The next day, Jackie and Mrs. Khrushchev lunched at Pallavicini Palace while outside in the small, cobblestoned square a thousand women had gathered yelling "Jah–kee, Jah–kee." Finally Mrs. Khrushchev guided Jackie to the window, took her hand and held it aloft. She too was joining the salute.

Jackie, a lifelong horsewoman, also attended a special performance held for her benefit at Vienna's famed Lippizaner Riding School. Dressed in a dark blue suit adorned by a triple string of pearls and wearing a white pill-box hat, she sat through two hours watching the incredible performance and discipline of these white Lippizaner Stallions, rarely seen outside of Vienna. I believe it was the highlight of her trip, Nikita Khrushchev notwithstanding. I always thought that Jackie preferred horses to most politicians.

Then we were off to London, where no duties awaited. Lee, Jackie's sister, had planned a grand party around the christening at her home, a mews house, at Number 4 Buckingham Place. The party was to be an intimate and charming affair and the guests were to include Prime Minister Harold Macmillan, Douglas Fairbanks Jr. and many stars of government, politics and screen. The President, still shaken by his meetings with Khrushchev, would finally get a chance to relax. But before the party was to take place, I would have my own cross to bear.

The christening of Lee's child was to take place in the crypt of London's Roman Catholic Westminster Cathedral. Because this was a private event, no press was to be allowed. But the announcement of this unofficial and private visit had been broadcast around the world, and some 2,000 newsmen and women and a few hundred photographers were gathered outside the cathedral. I was to photograph the christening only for

Jackie with her daughter Caroline and her kittens relaxes on the lawn of the Kennedy compound. Although the First Lady, she remained simple and uncomplicated.

HYANNIS PORT, MASSACHUSETTS. SUMMER 1961

the eyes of the Kennedy and Radziwill families. Yet knowing that the world's press was clamoring for photographs, I pleaded with Jackie to release at least one picture of the christening. She refused. I then pleaded with JFK, who agreed with me, but he acquiesced to Jackie's wish for privacy. For me, of course, the problem was that I knew I would be hated by my peers, and in addition would be accused of having made a multi-million-dollar deal—which I had not done, nor even considered. But there was to be no release of even a single photograph.

The christening in the lightless crypt went off simply enough with the President dutifully holding two-foot candles, signing the register and looking generally ill at ease. But the setting was bizarre, given the stark, almost medieval feeling of that vault-like room furnished with gilded, satin-covered chairs and settees instead of the usual wooden benches. This was due, I suppose, to the supreme celebrity of the occasion, with the President of the United States and his wife, assisted by a group of curious priests and nuns, delivering the standard rights and prayers of a normal baptism.

I had been ushered into the cathedral by both the Secret Service and Scotland Yard, out of sight of the assembled press. The trick now was to get me to Lee's home, quite a distance from the cathedral. So I was taken in hand by Scotland Yard, and many a homeowner was startled as the Yard men took me over roofs and through people's gardens and backyards, with all my cameras and a tripod. I finally arrived at Lee's house through the rear, somewhat out of breath, but again unseen by the press, who were camped out in force outside of the house in that narrow London mews.

On that same day in the summer of 1961, Caroline has come out of the bush playing "hide and seek."

HYANNIS PORT, MASSACHUSETTS. SUMMER 1961

XII

By mid 1962, as far as I was concerned, I had finished my assignment to document the Kennedy administration. By then I had photographed all conceivable presidential and staff conferences from intimate strategy events to meetings of the cabinet and joint chiefs of staff. I had covered the department heads from the secretaries of state and defense to treasury and labor. I had spent tens of hours with the President alone and covered the White House and the family at work and at play, with the play part, the personal part, becoming more and more difficult as Jackie became increasingly preoccupied with her privacy, even in the summers at Hyannis Port. I had amassed nearly 40,000 negatives. It was time to get back to New York.

I had reopened my studio, returning to Washington only occasionally to cover a special event or respond to a special request by the President or the First Lady, until that fateful day in November of 1963.

Like everyone else in the country, in the world, I still acutely feel that day's heartbreaking tragedy. I had completed a Volkswagen ad in the morning involving a woman driver and her canine companion, a Great Dane. That afternoon I was to photograph a group of black musicians from the film *The Pawnbroker*, for which I had been contracted to do the stills. I walked out of Central Park down Sixth Avenue when I noticed something peculiar. Traffic on the avenue had stopped and cars, parked at the curb, were surrounded by clusters of people. I walked up to one of these groups to ask what was happening. "The President has been shot." "What President?" I replied, unable to comprehend the implication. "President Kennedy," he answered. I can still feel my blood freezing, and the cold gripping my spine. I ran down the avenue to my studio and realized on arrival, when I saw the black musicians in tears, that our beloved President was dead, killed by a madman in an insane act of his-

The First Lady descends the stairs of the Elysée Palace, home of the French President, where she had just charmed General de Gaulle, an otherwise dour and imposing figure. Before leaving Paris, Jackie would become the toast of the town.

PARIS. JUNE 1961

tory, the first of others to follow. I went down to Washington that night and checked in at the White House. I was with Pierre Salinger and the rest of the White House staff when we saw the assassin murdered as well, before a large crowd of people and in front of dozens of television cameras, by yet another madman. And I went to the Capitol to photograph the silent mass of Americans, standing in line by the thousands and for many hours, to catch a final glimpse and pay their last respects to the President in his coffin. And the next morning I watched Jackie and her children and Bobby and the world's leaders walk in solemn step to mourn their slain leader. I watched Jackie all dressed in black, a veil covering her face, and I admired her incredible courage. I photographed with great difficulty, knowing that the world had changed, not for the better, but for the worse. And five years later, after Martin Luther King and finally my close friend Bobby, met the same fate, I left the country, not to return for eighteen years.

I saw Jackie only twice over the years, once running into her on the street and once at a party. She too had left the country and returned to begin a new and very different life as an editor. But to many she still represented those lost years, all that hope and enthusiasm and youth, the knowledge that ours was a great country, that we couldn't fail. She represented Camelot, became Camelot.

Our conversation was very friendly, though formal and awkward. Too much had happened, and I think the spark had left both of us.

When she died, all kinds of pictures flashed through my mind. A grinning Khrushchev, beside himself, like a love-struck kid in her presence. A normally solemn and remote DeGaulle unbending his six–foot–four frame in a rare smile while talking to her in his language. A proud John

The party to honor the Kennedys in Paris was the city's party of the year. The icons of high society were fighting for invitations to the event. Here Jackie, accompanied by Mrs. Charles de Gaulle, is appraised by Parisians.

PARIS. JUNE 1961

115

F. Kennedy presenting her to his assembled family all over again on the day he was elected President. A regal First Lady welcoming the Shah of Iran to the White House. A gentle First Lady welcoming Pablo Casals, the cellist, who had not set foot in America for many years. The tender, loving mother reading to her children.

She will always be a part of me, that young, naive photographer, full of wonder and expectations. She will always be a part of America, and the world. Jackie and Jack both.

Jackie looked absolutely stunning at that ball. Those who were there still talk about the event.

PARIS. JUNE 1961

Eulogy

Last summer, when we were on the upper deck on the boat at the Vineyard, waiting for President and Mrs. Clinton to arrive, Jackie turned to me and said: "Teddy, you go down and greet the President."

But I said: "Maurice (Tempelsman) is already there."

And Jackie answered: "Teddy, you do it. Maurice isn't running for re-election."

She was always there—for all our family—in her special way.

She was a blessing to us and to the nation, and a lesson to the world on how to do things right, how to be a mother, how to appreciate history, how to be courageous.

No one else looked like her, spoke like her, wrote like her or was so original in the way she did things. No one we knew ever had a better sense of self.

The meeting between the young President and Chairman Khrushchev had been bitter. Khrushchev had tried to bully and threaten JFK, who had remained calm. But that night at Schloss Schoenbrunn a different Nikita emerged. Totally captivated by Jackie, he could hardly contain his enthusiasm, bubbling over with charm and anecdotes.

VIENNA. JUNE 1961

Eight months before she married Jack, they went together to President Eisenhower's inaugural ball. Jackie said later that that's where they decided they like inaugurations.

No one ever gave more meaning to the title of First Lady. The nation's capital city looks as it does because of her. She saved Lafayette Square and Pennsylvania Avenue.

Jackie brought the greatest artists to the White House, and brought the arts to the center of national attention. Today, in large part because of her inspiration and vision, the arts are an abiding part of national policy.

President Kennedy took such delight in her brilliance and her spirit. At a White House dinner, he once leaned over and told the wife of the French ambassador, "Jackie speaks fluent French. But I only understand one out of every five words she says—and that word is DeGaulle."

And then, during those four endless days in 1963, she held us together as a family and a country. In large part because of her, we could grieve and then go on. She lifted us up and, in the doubt and darkness, she gave her fellow citizens back their pride as Americans. She was then 34 years old.

The Kennedys came to London to officiate at the baptism of the Radziwill's newborn child. The President was to be the godfather. Here, at the party in their honor, the First Lady awaits her guests...and introduces the pill-box hat to the U.K.

LONDON, ENGLAND. JUNE 1961

Afterward, as the eternal flame she lit flickered in the autumn of Arlington Cemetery, Jackie went on to do what she most wanted—to raise Caroline and John, and warm her family's life and that of all the Kennedys.

Robert Kennedy sustained her, and she helped make it possible for Bobby to continue. She kept Jack's memory alive, as he carried Jack's mission on.

Her two children turned out to be extraordinary, honest, unspoiled and with a character equal to hers. And she did it in the most trying of circumstances. They are her two miracles.

Her love for Caroline and John was deep and unqualified. She reveled in their accomplishments, she hurt with their sorrows and she felt sheer joy and delight in spending time with them. At the mere mention of one of their names, Jackie's eyes would shine brighter and her smile would grow bigger.

She once said that if you "bungle raising your children, nothing else much matters in life." She didn't bungle. Once again, she showed us how to do the most important thing of all, and do it right.

At a party given by Prince Stanislas Radziwill and Jackie's sister Lee, and attended by the British Prime Minister and members of British high society, the theater and the press, Jackie again sparkled and was the true jewel of the gathering.

LONDON. JUNE 1961

When she went to work, Jackie became a respected professional in the world of publishing. And because of her, remarkable books came to life. She searched out new authors and ideas. She was interested in everything.

Her love of history became a devotion to historic preservation. You knew, when Jackie joined the cause to save a building in Manhattan, the bulldozers might as well turn around and go home.

She had a wonderful sense of humor—a way of focusing on someone with total attention—and a little-girl delight in who they were and what they were saying. It was a gift of herself that she gave to others. And in spite of all her heartache and loss, she never faltered.

I often think of what she said about Jack in December after he died: "They made him a legend, when he would have preferred to be a man." Jackie would have preferred just to be herself, but the world insisted that she be a legend, too.

She never wanted public notice—in part, I think, because it brought back painful memories of an unbearable sorrow, endured in the glare of a million lights.

Lee Radziwill, Jackie's younger sister, and her son Anthony on a visit to America during the summer of 1961.

HYANNIS PORT, MASSACHUSETTS. SUMMER 1961

In all the years since then, her genuineness and depth of character continued to shine through the privacy, and reach people everywhere. Jackie was too young to be a widow in 1963, and too young to die now.

Her grandchildren were bringing new joy to her life, a joy that illuminated her face whenever you saw them together. Whether it was taking Rose and Tatiana for an ice-cream cone, or taking a walk in Central Park with little Jack as she did last Sunday, she relished being Grand Jackie and showering her grandchildren with love.

At the end, she worried more about us than herself. She let her family and friends know she was thinking of them. How cherished were those wonderful notes in her distinctive hand on her powder-blue stationery!

In truth, she did everything she could—and more—for each of us.

She made a rare and noble contribution to the American spirit. But for us, most of all she was a magnificent wife, mother, grandmother, sister, aunt and friend.

She graced our history. And for those of us who knew and loved her— she graced our lives.

Senator Edward M. Kennedy

The five Kennedy women: Joan, Jean Kennedy Smith, Eunice Kennedy Shriver, Jackie and Ethel—on the porch of Ambassador Kennedy's home, known as "The Big House."

FOLLOWING PAGE

The funeral procession for President Kennedy passes on the way to Arlington Cemetery.

HYANNIS PORT, MASSACHUSETTS. AUGUST 1960

WASHINGTON, D.C. NOVEMBER 23, 1963